W9-AMS-253

THE SOUTHERN COLONIES:
The Search for Wealth (1600-1770)

TITLE LIST

THE SOUTHERN COLONIES:
The Search for Wealth (1600-1770)

BY TERESA LACLAIR

MASON CREST

Mason Crest
370 Reed Road
Broomall, Pennsylvania 19008
www.masoncrest.com

Copyright © 2013 by Mason Crest, an imprint of National Highlights, Inc. All rights reserved. No part of this publication may be reproduced or transmitted in any form or by any means, electronic or mechanical, including photocopying, recording, taping, or any information storage and retrieval system, without permission from the publisher.

Printed and bound in Hashemite Kingdom of Jordan.

First printing
9 8 7 6 5 4 3 2 1

            Library of Congress Cataloging-in-Publication Data

LaClair, Teresa.
  The southern colonies : the search for wealth (1600-1770) / by Teresa LaClair.
      p. cm. — (How America became America)
  Includes bibliographical references and index.
   ISBN 978-1-4222-2398-7 (hardcover) — ISBN 978-1-4222-2396-3 (hardcover series) ISBN 978-1-4222-9308-9 (ebook)
  1. Southern States—Economic conditions—17th century—Juvenile literature. 2. Southern States—Economic conditions—18th century—Juvenile literature. 3. Southern States—History—Colonial period, ca. 1600-1775—Juvenile literature. I. Title.
  F212.L34 2012
  975'.02—dc22
                        2011000581

Produced by Harding House Publishing Services, Inc.
www.hardinghousepages.com
Cover design by Torque Advertising + Design.

THE SOUTHERN COLONIES: THE SEARCH FOR WEALTH

1584–Sir Walter Raleigh sends Philip Amadas and Arthur Barlowe to look for a good place to start a colony on the North American coast. The men choose Roanoke Island, on the coast of what is now North Carolina.

May 14, 1607–The colonists of the Virginia Company arrive on Jamestown Island. Their goal is to find gold and a trade route across the country to the Pacific Ocean.

1585–Raleigh sends a group of men to settle on Roanoke Island. The men are mostly soldiers and scholars.

Winter 1609-1610–"The starving time." A hard winter and not enough food leaves only 60 of 504 people alive by spring.

1492–Christopher Columbus lands in the New World.

June 11, 1578– Queen Elizabeth I tells Sir Humphrey Gilbert to find New World lands for England.

Late Autumn 1609–Four hundred new colonists arrive in Jamestown.

1610-1614–First Anglo-Powhatan War begins. It is mainly Lord De La Warr's fault. He treats the Native Americans badly and makes them angry.

August 1587–One hundred and seventeen new colonists arrive at Roanoke, both men and women. They find the men left behind have been killed by Native Americans. Even so, the captain of the ship leaves them there.

August 18, 1590–John White returns to Roanoke. He finds that all the colonists have dis-appeared. Someone carved the word "Croatan" into wood, but no one knows for certain what happened to all the people.

1614–Sir Thomas Dale takes Pocahontas from her father, Powhatan. A deadly battle follows. Finally, Pocahontas mar-ries John Rolfe, ending the war between Native Americans and settlers.

1619–The House of Burgesses meets for the first time. It is the first type of government in the New World that allows people to vote for their leaders.

1649–The Toleration Act is passed in Maryland. It gives equal rights to people of all Christian faiths.

1729–North Carolina separates from South Carolina and becomes a royal colony.

1728–James Oglethorpe, an English member of parliament, wants to fix the problem of debtors' prisons in England. He supports the idea of starting a colony for debtors in the New World.

1749–The English government agrees to let the Georgia colonists own slaves.

1644-1646–Second Anglo-Powhatan War. It ends with the Native Americans being forced off their land in the Chesapeake Bay area.

1634–King Charles tells Calvert's oldest son, Cecil, to start a new colony. He names it Maryland.

1663–King Charles gives a huge piece of land to eight lords. The land makes up what we know today as North Carolina, South Carolina, and Georgia.

1732–King George II gives a group of men a twenty-one-year plan to start a colony in Georgia. Rules for the colony include bans on alcohol and slaves.

1752–The Georgia leaders give control of the colony back to the king.

1619–A Dutch ship trades twenty Africans to the Jamestown colonists in exchange for food.

1670–The English settle near what is now Charleston, South Carolina. The colonists come from the Barbados colony, bringing their black slaves with them.

February 1733–James Oglethorpe and thirty-five families arrive in Georgia. They start the city of Savannah.

7

Chapter One
THE FIRST AMERICAN COLONIES

In 1492, Christopher Columbus sailed west from Spain. He landed on the islands we call the Bahamas. He went back to Europe then. He told everyone about his journey. For the first time, people in Europe learned about the land to the west. Nobody had imagined a whole new continent was there. Now more explorers sailed west. People came looking for gold or other riches.

North America and South America were not empty, though. Millions of people lived there. In South America were the Aztec, the Maya, and other groups. In North America, there were hundreds of **Native** tribes.

When the Europeans arrived, they spread sicknesses to the people of the Americas. The Natives couldn't handle the new diseases. They were not used to the new germs. Nobody knows exactly how many people died from diseases like **smallpox**

Native people are people who have lived in a place for a long time.

Smallpox is a disease that was brought to America from Europe.

DID COLUMBUS DISCOVER AMERICA?

People sometimes say that Columbus "discovered" America. You can't really "discover" a place where millions of people already lived! Europeans called America a New World—but for the Native people who already lived there, it was just "the world."

and **measles**. About nine out of every ten people died within the first hundred years after the Europeans arrived.

The first Europeans to arrive and set up **colonies** in the **New World** were the Spanish. They claimed large parts of South America and some of southern North America.

In England, people were not as interested yet in building colonies. They had other things to think about. People there were fighting over religion. Then Elizabeth I became queen in 1558. Things became calmer.

Measles is a sickness that was not very dangerous in Europe, but killed many Native people in America.

Colonies are places where people from another country have come to make a new home.

The **New World** is North, Central, and South America.

When Europeans arrived in the Americas, they were surprised by the way the Native people lived. They dressed differently and talked differently. Sometimes, Europeans were willing to learn from the Natives—but other times they were afraid of them or fought with them.

The relationship between England and Spain, though, was getting worse. When Ireland fought against English rule, Spain helped them fight. When the Netherlands fought the Spanish, England joined in.

At the same time, the English were getting nervous about the Spanish colonies. They were afraid Spain was getting too powerful. They worried that Spain might spread its colonies across all of North and South America.

This reenactment shows Queen Elizabeth talking to Sir Walter Raleigh about his voyage to Virginia.

When the English landed in the new land, they did not know much about how to live there. They were used to living in England, where things were very different.

To make sure Spain didn't claim all the New World, England decided to build its own colony there. Queen Elizabeth sent Sir Walter Raleigh, a soldier and explorer, to build it. She told him to take all the land between the Spanish colonies in the south and the French colonies in the north. He named the area Virginia.

In 1585, a group of one hundred men arrived on Roanoke Island (in what is now North Carolina). Some of the men were soldiers. Others had come to study the new land.

13

Soon, the colony started having problems. A lot of the men were used to having servants. They didn't know how to work hard. They missed their soft beds and fancy food. They didn't like having to find their own food.

At first, the Natives in the area were friendly to the Englishmen. They showed the newcomers how to make fish traps. They traded food for tools. For a while, the colonists

Roanoke settlement

14

didn't have to find their own food. They could eat the supplies they had brought with them or the food they got from the Natives.

Then, a silver cup disappeared from the colony. When the Englishmen found out that one of the Natives had taken it, they were very angry. One of them burned down the Native village as revenge.

After that, the Natives stopped being friendly to the colonists. They stopped helping the Englishmen find food. Instead, they destroyed the fish traps the colonists had made.

By spring, the Englishmen just wanted to go home. One man, Sir Richard Grenville, had gone back to England earlier in the fall. He was supposed to come back with more supplies, but he hadn't arrived.

In June, Sir Francis Drake, the famous English sea captain, arrived at the colony. The people there didn't want to wait for Grenville any longer. They left with Drake and went back to England.

The next year, in 1587, Sir Walter Raleigh sent another group of colonists to Virginia. This group had both men and women. The first group had gone to the

Sir Francis Drake

15

THE DEFEAT OF THE SPANISH ARMADA

As part of England's war against Spain, Queen Elizabeth told English sea captains to attack Spanish ships. Spanish ships coming back from New World colonies sometimes carried treasure. England wanted that treasure. More important, England didn't want Spain to have the treasure.

The Spanish king, Philip II, was very angry that the English were attacking his ships. He decided to take care of the problem. In 1588, he sent his armada of 130 ships to attack England.

Spain wanted to destroy England's power. Instead, things went badly for Spain. First, they hit a bad storm. Then, when they attacked, the English ships were quicker and could turn faster. Most of the Spanish ships were sunk.

Spain lost a lot of its power with the defeat of its armada. The English people felt good. They had defeated their biggest enemy.

New World to study and explore. This group, though, arrived ready to build homes, plant crops, and settle down.

A few days after they got to Roanoke, one of the women, Eleanor Dare, had a baby. She named the little girl Virginia. Virginia Dare was the first English baby born in the New World.

Eleanor Dare's father, John White, was supposed to be the colony's governor. When his granddaughter Virginia was ten days old, White left with the ship's captain to go

The Lost Colony (a reenactment)

back to England. He was going to get more supplies and come right back to Roanoke.

But things didn't work out the way John White wanted. England's war with Spain had gotten worse, and White couldn't find a ship to take him back to the colony.

Three years later, White was finally able to get a ship and supplies. He sailed back to Roanoke. He was looking forward to seeing his family again.

When John White got to Roanoke, though, he didn't see what he expected. Instead of a busy colony, there was silence. Instead of neat buildings and fields, there was only a high fence. There were no houses at all.

White searched and searched, but he couldn't find any sign of the colonists. The only clue was the word CROATOAN carved on a tree.

John White thought that maybe the colonists had moved south to Croatoan Island, but he couldn't find them there, either. Eventually, he had to leave and go back to England. He wanted to make another trip to keep looking, but he was never able to. He died three years later. He never found out what had happened to the Roanoke colony.

Today, hundreds of years later, people still don't know what happened. Where did the colonists go? People who study history have some ideas about what might have happened. Natives might have killed the colonists. Or they might have joined a local tribe. Nobody knows for sure.

The Roanoke colony was only the beginning, though. Soon, England would start another colony in Virginia. This one would be more successful.

John White returns to Roanoke colony to find it deserted. The only clue, the word "Croatoan" carved into a tree.

Chapter Two
THE JAMESTOWN SETTLEMENT

In the spring of 1607, 108 settlers arrived in Virginia. They landed on Jamestown Island, sixty miles inland from the Chesapeake Bay. The men, women, and children had been sent by the Virginia Company to start a new colony. The Virginia Company had agreed to pay for the trip. In return, the colonists would give the company part of the money they earned. They planned to find gold. They also expected to make a lot of money from trade.

Not long after they arrived, a group of Natives attacked the settlers. The local Natives had learned that the Europeans were not always friendly. The colonists fought them and then built a fort. The fort was shaped like a triangle. It had high wooden walls. The storehouse, church, and houses were inside.

The colony had other troubles besides the Natives. While some people helped out and worked hard, other people didn't want to work. They wanted to find gold, get rich, and go back to England. Some of the men went out every day looking for gold (which they never found). They didn't help the colony at all.

Building Fort James

The Virginia Company didn't actually care much about the survival of the colony either. They had started the colony with the idea of quick money. Now they were impatient. They wanted the money to start coming in quickly. But that wasn't happening.

One of the colonists, John Smith, was frustrated with the Virginia Company. He was frustrated with many of the other colonists as well. He wanted to make Jamestown a real community. He wished everyone would settle down and focus on finding food instead of treasure.

A few months after the colonists had arrived, John Smith was out looking for food when Powhatan, the chief of the local Native tribe, captured him. For a month, Smith stayed with Powhatan. They became friends. Powhatan's twelve-year-old daughter, Pocahontas, became friends with Smith as well.

In January 1608, John Smith left Powhatan and went back to Jamestown. Things had gotten worse while he had been gone. The people were hungry and unhappy. Smith was able to calm everybody down. He set up trade with Powhatan's people. Pocahontas acted as messenger and go-between for her father and the Jamestown colonists.

Trading with the Indians

23

In September, the colonists elected John Smith as the head of the colony. Smith made decisions that helped Jamestown grow. The people started farming. Everyone helped out.

Then, in the fall of 1609, two bad things happened. First, John Smith was hurt when a bag of **gunpowder** exploded. He had to go back to England for medical treatment. That left Jamestown without its leader.

The second thing that happened was that another ship arrived, filled with four hundred new colonists.

The people in Jamestown probably would have had enough food for the winter if it hadn't been for the new arrivals. After all, they had been farming, and they had gotten some food through Pocahontas and Powhatan. Now, though, they had nowhere near enough. The people of Jamestown called that winter the "starving time." Of the 504 colonists who started the winter, only 60 lived to see spring.

By spring, everyone who was left just wanted to go back to England. They left Jamestown and sailed downriver toward the Chesapeake Bay. Just as they reached the bay, though, they met another ship. The ship carried supplies and a new governor, Lord De La Warr. De La Warr insisted the Jamestown colonists turn around and sail back upriver. The colony was not going to be abandoned after all.

De La Warr was not a kind man. He made very strict rules for the colony. He also didn't think much of the Natives in the area. He burned Native houses and fields. A war started between the colonists and Powhatan. Eventually, one of the colonists, John Rolfe, married Pocahontas. This ended the war. The two communities once more lived in peace.

Despite the problems, Jamestown grew. Slowly, other settlements were built in nearby areas.

Gunpowder is a mixture of chemicals that explodes when around fire or heat.

Without enough food, the settlers grew sick and weak.

The settlers began to grow tobacco. John Rolfe, the husband of Pocahontas, was the first to grow tobacco. He experimented with varieties from the Caribbean and from the local area. When he sent some of the tobacco back to England, people there liked it. They asked for more.

25

Many of the settlers died during their first year in the new land.

Now everyone wanted to grow tobacco. People in Virginia planted larger and larger crops. That meant they needed more land. It also meant they needed people to work in the fields. In order to get people to the area, the Virginia Company started using **indentured servants**. The company would pay for a person to travel to Jamestown. In return, that person would agree to work for the company for several years. This way of getting to the New World became so popular that hundreds of thousands of people—mostly young, unmarried men—arrived during the years to come.

Indentured servants agreed to work for a boss for a certain amount of time, after which they were free.

26

Growing tobacco in Jamestown

The need for people to work in the tobacco fields also led to the beginning of slave labor in America. The first slaves arrived in 1619 on board a Dutch ship. At first, the Africans were treated the same as indentured servants. They still had some rights. People thought of them as human beings. Over the next fifty years, though, the Africans and their children lost any rights they once had in Virginia. The colony passed laws that drew a line between black and white servants. Blacks were no longer thought of as equal human beings.

As Jamestown and the towns around it grew, the colonies began to make more of their own laws. They were still loyal to England and the king. But England was far away, on the other side of the ocean. The people in Virginia governed themselves the way they liked. They enjoyed having their freedom.

27

Noua TERRAE-MARIAE tabula

This Northerne part of Virginia (the limitts whereof extend farther Southwards,) is heere inserted for the better description of the entrance into the Bay of Chesapeack.

VIRGINIAE PARS

CHE · SA · PE · ACK · bay

James towne

Point Comfort
Yorke flu.
Charles R.
C. Henry

OCEANVS ORIENTALIS

Sea Leagues

C. Charles
Accomack
Smiths Island
Sommerset C.
Matopongue flu.
Matopongue
Fenhes Isle
Swansecut Creek
Chingoteaq Isle

Potowmeck

Portobacke
Ecker Poynt
Sicklemore Isle
Heron Islande
Charles C.
Patuxent flu.
S.ta Maria
Calvert C.
S. Michaells poynt
S. Gregories poynt
Anne-Arundell C.
Matopanian
Patuxent

Kent C.
Dorchester C.
Talbot C.
Wicomico
Cecill
Sasquahanaq flu.
The Isles
Sasquehannocks

Piscatoway

Baltemore County

Delaware Bay

Noua Iersy Pars

NOV. ANGLI. PARS

The Atchievment of the Right Honourable Cecilius Calvert Baron Baltemore & Baltemore Absolute Lord and Proprietary of the Provinces of Maryland, and Avalon

FATTI MASCHII, PAROLE FEMI.

Ogilby-Lond 1671

Chapter Three
MARYLAND

During the 1600s, when most of the American colonies were built, a person's religion mattered a lot to other people. Pretty much all the colonists were Christian, but different types of Christians disagreed with each other. Whether a person was Protestant or Roman Catholic was a very big deal. Back in Europe, Protestants and Catholics had been fighting each other for more than a hundred years. Each side thought the other was completely wrong. They disagreed so strongly they even killed each other.

People looking for religious freedom had built the northern American colonies, like Massachusetts and Connecticut. These people were called **Puritans**. They were

People who are **Protestant** belong to Christian religions that broke away from the Roman Catholic Church.

People who are **Roman Catholic** are Christians whose religious leader is the Pope in Rome.

Puritans were people who believed that the official Church of England was too much like the Catholic Church and needed to be stricter.

Protestants who thought the Anglican Church hadn't changed enough when it had broken away from the Roman Catholic Church.

For a long time, England went back and forth between Protestant and Roman Catholic rulers. When a Protestant king or queen ruled the nation, life was difficult for Roman Catholics. The opposite was also true—when a Roman Catholic king or queen ruled, life was tough for Protestants. Finally, though, the country decided to stay Protestant.

In the early 1600s, a man named George Calvert lived in England. He worked for the king and the king liked him. Things were going well for Calvert, until he became a Roman Catholic. As a Catholic, Calvert was not allowed to work for the king anymore. Because the king liked him, though, he made Calvert Lord Baltimore. He gave Calvert land in Ireland.

Ireland was a beautiful place, but Calvert was not happy there. Five years earlier, he had bought a piece of land in Newfoundland in the New World. He had sent people to build a colony there. He had never visited the colony himself, though. Now, he decided to move to Newfoundland.

In 1628, he moved to Newfoundland. His wife and nine of his children went with him. Forty settlers went too. Calvert's colony was called Avalon.

For nearly two years, Calvert lived in Avalon with his family. Life was not easy there. He had to deal with French ships raiding their supplies. He also had to deal with the colony's Protestant leaders spreading rumors about him. Calvert wanted Avalon to be a place where everyone was welcome. He wanted Roman Catholics to feel welcome as well as Protestants. This didn't happen, though.

Finally, Calvert had had enough. He wanted to leave. The final straw had been the winter of 1628–1629. The winter had held on until May. Nothing would grow. The water in the bay froze. People were hungry and sick. Nearly a dozen people died. Calvert's wife,

especially, hated Avalon and wanted to leave.

Calvert's first idea was to move to Jamestown and settle there. Because he was a Roman Catholic, though, the colony would not let him live there.

Calvert went back to England. He talked to King Charles about what had happened. King Charles still liked Calvert. He wanted to help his friend. He promised Calvert (Lord Baltimore) a large piece of land north of Virginia. The king called the area Maryland. He named it after the queen, Henrietta Maria.

Calvert's idea for Maryland was that it would be a place where Roman Catholics could live and be safe. In Maryland, Catholics would be able to go to church without a problem. Nobody would be mean to them because of their religion.

Sir George Calvert, the first Lord Baltimore

31

Cecil Calvert

Then, in 1632, Calvert died. King Charles hadn't actually given him the **charter** to Maryland yet. The king didn't want Calvert's dream to die with him, though. He gave the charter to Calvert's son, Cecil Calvert. The charter said that the colony needed to send the king one-fifth of any gold and silver found. Every year, they also needed to send two Native arrows.

Cecil Calvert was not able to move to Maryland himself. Instead, he wrote up a list of instructions for the new colonists. He sent his brother, Leonard Calvert, to the colony, along with several hundred settlers.

Leonard Calvert served as the first governor of Maryland. As governor, he had a lot of power. When Calvert arrived in Maryland, he gave land to all the settlers who had come with him. He gave large pieces of land to

A **charter** is the legal right of ownership of land that is given by the king.

32

many of his friends and relatives. Other settlers received smaller farms on those **estates**. The people on the smaller farms paid rent to the owner of the estate. The estate owners paid rent to Calvert.

Maryland had been built with the idea that it would be a place where Catholics could be free to worship. England was a Protestant country, though. Calvert needed to let Protestants settle in Maryland, too. Soon, Maryland had more Protestants than Catholics.

Calvert and the other Roman Catholics worried that the Protestants might take over. They worried Catholics might end up being treated badly after all.

To make sure this didn't happen, in 1649, Maryland passed the Toleration Act. The Toleration Act said that all Christians would have the same legal rights. It wouldn't matter if they were Roman Catholic, Protestant, or another Christian group. Even though this doesn't sound like much today, it was a big deal at the time. Even though it left out people who weren't Christian (like the Natives), it was a big step toward religious freedom.

The Toleration Act did not last, however. A few years after it had been passed, a group of Puritans took control of the Maryland government. They got rid of the Toleration Act. They burned down most of the Catholic churches.

In 1658, Calvert took back control of Maryland. He made the Toleration Act the law again. By the end of the 1600s, though, Maryland had become much more Protestant. The Maryland government got rid of the Toleration Act once again.

Even though Calvert's dream for his colony didn't exactly come true, it was still important. The Toleration Act didn't last, but it was an important step toward religious freedom. The ideas in the Toleration Act would later be used to help write the United States Constitution.

Estates are large amounts of land owned by one person.

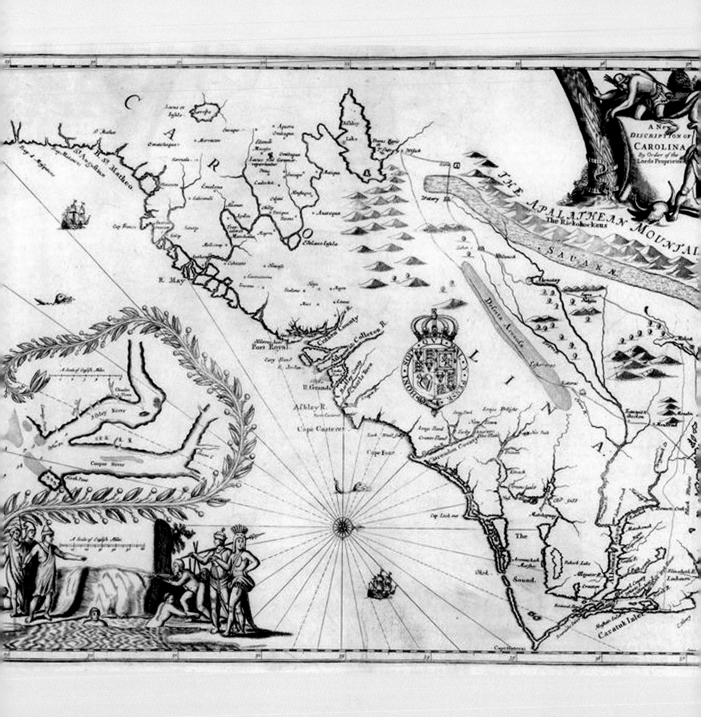

A New DISCRIPTION OF CAROLINA By Order of the Lords Proprietors

Chapter Four
THE CAROLINAS

A few small groups of people had come to the Carolinas during the 1650s. They had left other North American colonies and moved south. The Carolinas weren't an official colony at that time, but England had claimed the area. Many of the people there were trying to find more freedom than they had in the Northern colonies.

King Charles wanted to have more power in North America. He was worried the Spanish might move north and take over. In 1663, the king gave a charter to eight of his closest friends. The charter put the eight men in charge of the Carolinas. They would be called the Lord Proprietors.

The Lord Proprietors would have a lot of power in the new colony. They planned on following something called the Grand Model. The Grand Model was a plan a **philosopher** named John Locke had written. Under the Grand Model, the land would be divided into counties. An **earl** and two **barons** would govern each county.

A **philosopher** is someone who thinks and writes about ideas.

Earls and **barons** are names for aristocratic rulers.

35

Tenants would live in the counties and farm the land. The idea was to make the Carolinas a kind of **aristocracy**. It would have **lords** and **peasants**. It would be the kind of place that had existed in England in the **Middle Ages**. It would be better than England in the Middle Ages, though. King Charles and the Lord Proprietors hoped the Grand Model would make the Carolinas into the kind of place that had only existed in stories.

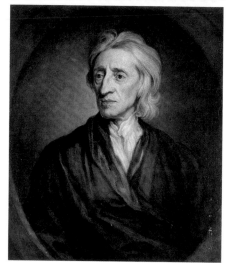

John Locke

The Grand Model didn't work out as they had hoped, though. The Lord Proprietors had imagined themselves ruling over a land of rolling green hills and tiny farms. The land was nothing like this. Instead of meadows, there were thick forests. Instead of farmland, there were swamps.

The Grand Model did not work at all. The settlers thought it was a silly idea. They weren't interested in being ruled by lords. They weren't interested in suddenly being

Tenants are people who rent, but do not own, the land they live on.

An **aristocracy** is a country ruled by a group of rich families.

Lords are rich people who rule over other people, and usually own the land everyone else lives on.

Peasants are the poorer people who live on and farm the lord's land.

The **Middle Ages** (500-1500) was that time in Europe when lords ruled over the land and the peasants.

thought of as peasants. They had come to North America to find freedom. They wanted a new life. They didn't want to be ruled by lords!

The Grand Model didn't think about the rights of the ordinary people. The ordinary people were the ones who built the North American colonies, though. The plan didn't work because it wasn't **realistic**. Even though it didn't work, the Lord Proprietors were still in control of the colony for years.

An early portrayal of slavery

In the 1670s, many settlers started arriving in the Carolinas. Most of these came from Barbados, an island to the south in the Caribbean Sea. In Barbados, a lot of people had gotten rich from huge sugar **plantations**. Other people wanted to grow sugarcane and get rich, too. Barbados didn't have enough land for everyone, though. When people got to Barbados and realized there wasn't room for them, some of them moved on to the Carolinas.

Realistic means something that could easily happen.

Plantations are large farms, usually growing one kind of crop, and often worked by slaves.

37

As people came to the Carolinas, many brought slaves with them. In Barbados, slaves who had been captured in Africa now worked on the sugar plantations. The settlers in the Carolinas used slaves, too. They also captured Native people to use as slaves. In the Carolinas, the slave trade began at the same time the settlement did.

In the Carolinas, people usually ended up growing rice instead of sugarcane. The swamps were good places for rice to grow. Growing rice was hard work, though. Working in the swamps was hard on people. Mosquitoes lived there. The mosquitoes carried diseases like malaria and yellow fever. The white people who worked on the rice plantations caught these diseases. Many of the whites did not live very long. The plantation owners discovered that Africans did not catch these kinds of diseases as easily. They brought in lots of African slaves to work on the rice plantations.

The African workers lived longer than the white workers, but lots of them still died. Most of the plantation owners didn't take care of their workers. Instead of trying to make sure the workers were safe and healthy and had enough food, the owners just let them die. They thought it was cheaper to buy new slaves than it was to look after the people

This drawing shows how tightly packed African people were in the ships that brought them to America.

38

they had. Because so many slaves died, the owners always wanted new ones. This meant the slave trade kept going for years.

North and South Carolina were all one colony in the 1600s. Still, they were very different places. The huge plantations were nearly all in the area that is now South Carolina. North Carolina was more of a wilderness. People moved north to get away from the plantation owners in the south. Or else they moved to North Carolina from other parts of North America.

The settlers in North Carolina were usually people who wanted freedom. They were **independent** folk. Most of them had small farms or lived off the land as hunters. North Carolina was thought of as a place where ordinary people could be free. It was a place where most people considered themselves equal. This did not mean they treated *everyone* as equals, though. They treated the Natives just as badly as most of the other colonies did. The settlers killed or drove away most of the Native Americans.

In 1712, the Carolinas were officially divided into North and South Carolina. The Lord Proprietors still ruled both sections, though. The people of North Carolina weren't very happy about being ruled by the Lord Proprietors. In 1719, they rebelled. The next year, England sent a governor to lead North Carolina. The Lord Proprietors still had some control, though, since they got to appoint the governor.

Finally, in 1729, the British government took over from the Lord Proprietors. For the next several decades, the Carolinas would be governed much like the other American colonies.

People who are **independent** like to think for themselves and don't like to be controlled by other people.

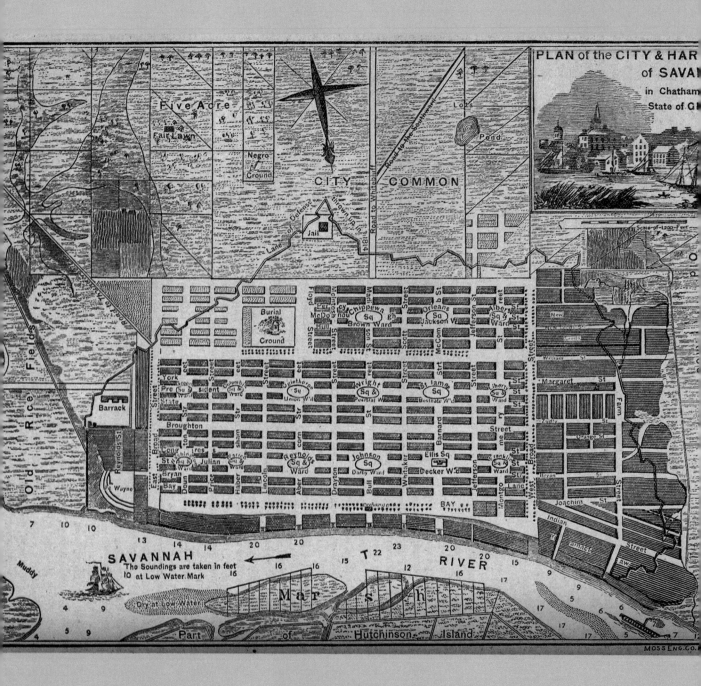

PLAN of the CITY & HAR[BOR]
of SAVAN[NAH]
in Chatham [County]
State of G[eorgia]

Chapter Five
GEORGIA

What happened hundreds of years ago if people couldn't pay the money they owed? A lot of times, they were sent to debtors' prison. Debtors' prison was a miserable place. It was often damp and dirty. Too many people lived in a small space. People couldn't leave until they'd paid the money they owed. Since they couldn't usually make money while in prison, their friends and relatives had to pay the money for them.

In 1728, a British politician named James Oglethorpe visited a debtors' prison in England. One of his best friends had been thrown into the prison. Oglethorpe was horrified. His friend was locked in a tiny cell with a man who was sick with smallpox. Soon, his friend got smallpox too. Then his friend died. Oglethorpe was mad. He wanted to do something to make things better.

Then Oglethorpe got an idea. Some of the land along the coast of North America still hadn't been settled. Britain was still worried about Spain in Florida. They still worried that Spain might decide to move north. Oglethorpe suggested that Britain build a new colony between South Carolina and Florida. The new colony would be called Georgia. It would be named after King George II. Georgia would be a debtors' colony. Instead of sending people to prison if they couldn't pay the money they owed, they could choose to go to Georgia.

King George agreed with the idea. In 1732, he gave a charter to a group of **trustees**. These people would be in charge of the colony for twenty-one years. After that, the king would take over again. While the trustees were in charge, they could make all the laws for Georgia. The people who lived there wouldn't be able to have a say in how they were governed. Everyone would get a piece of land, though. They wouldn't have to pay rent on the land for ten years.

The laws in Georgia would be a little different from the laws in the other American colonies. Because Georgia was set up to be a debtors' colony, Britain would help pay most of the colony's expenses. Also, slavery would be illegal. Alcohol would be illegal, too.

Portrait of James Oglethorpe

In February 1733, Oglethorpe arrived in Georgia with thirty-five families. Oglethorpe was going to be the first governor of the new colony.

The idea for a debtors' colony didn't really work out. North America could be a dangerous place. Building a new colony took a lot of hard work. That's why most of

Trustees are a group of people who run things as a group.

42

the debtors who had the chance to go to Georgia didn't want to go. They thought they would probably do better in prison. They hoped their families and friends could get them out soon. Then they could go back to living a comfortable life. They didn't want to go to Georgia and have to build a whole new life. Only eleven families of debtors actually agreed to move to Georgia.

At first, the colony grew very slowly. Some people didn't want to move there because they didn't like the strict laws. Many of the settlers who did go to Georgia were looking for a place where they could practice their religion freely. Back in Europe, these people

weren't able to worship the way they believed they should. Some of them, like the Salzburgers from Austria, had been kicked out of their own countries because of their religion. In Georgia, all Christians—except Roman Catholics—had the same legal rights.

Missionaries also went to Georgia. These missionaries had strong ideas about religion. They wanted to share their ideas with the settlers. One of these missionaries, John Wesley,

John Wesley, founder of the Methodist Chucrch.

Missionaries are people who travel to new places to teach people about religion.

arrived in Georgia in 1735. Wesley's first idea was to preach to the Native people. Instead, Oglethorpe asked him to be a pastor to the European settlers. The settlers were just getting started. They could use someone to help them.

Wesley didn't do well as a pastor for the Georgia settlers, though. Later, Wesley would start the Methodist Church, but at this point he was still an Anglican minister. Wesley tried to make the church in Georgia a fancy Anglican church. This didn't make sense for

FREDERICA RIVER

Fort Frederica on St. Simons Island where Oglethorpe lived the last six years of his stay in Georgia.

the time and place. The people were just annoyed with Wesley. They needed someone to teach them about how to live in this wild new place. Wesley just told them all the things they were doing wrong. He had arguments with the people. Most of the settlers didn't like him. Eventually, Wesley gave up and went back to Britain.

In general, most of the settlers weren't happy in Georgia. They didn't like the law that said they couldn't drink alcohol. They didn't like that they weren't allowed to buy land and make their farms bigger. They didn't like that they couldn't buy slaves. Before long, they changed the laws.

In 1752—nearly two years before the twenty-one-year deadline—the trustees gave up control of Georgia. Quickly, the colony started to look like all the other American colonies. The king appointed a governor. The settlers chose people to lead them. More and more people started moving to the area.

In less than twenty-five years after Oglethorpe had his idea, Georgia was doing well. It didn't look much like Oglethorpe's idea, though. Instead, it looked pretty much like all the other American colonies.

The thirteen American colonies were starting to form their own **identity**. They had new ideas about government. They had exciting thoughts about independence. It was these new ideas and thoughts that would soon lead to the Revolutionary War.

An **identity** is the way a group of people feels about themselves and who they are.

FIND OUT MORE

In Books

Coleman, Brooke. *The Colony of Georgia*. New York, N.Y.: The Rosen Publishing Group, 2000.

Harkins. Susan and William Harkins. *Colonial Virginia*. Hockessin, Del.: Mitchell Lane Publishers, 2005.

Isaacs, Sally. *Life on a Southern Plantation*. Chicago, Ill.: Reed Educational & Professional Publishing, 2000.

Niz, Xavier. *The Mystery of the Roanoke Colony*. Mankato, Minn.: Capstone Press, 2007.

Sita, Lisa. *Pocahontas: The Powhatan Culture and the Jamestown Colony*. New York, N.Y.: The Rosen Publishing Group, 2005.

Ward, Nancy. *Sir Walter Raleigh: Founding the Virginia Colony*. New York, N.Y.: Crabtree Publishing, Co., 2007.

On the Internet

Colonial Georgia
ourgeorgiahistory.com/history101/gahistory03.html

Colonial Williamsburg
www.colonialwilliamsburg.com/?WT.mc_id=663

History of the Southern Colonies
www.kidinfo.com/american_history/colonization_s_colonies.html

Indentured Servants
www.historyforkids.org/learn/northamerica/after1500/economy/indentured.htm

North Carolina Museum of History
ncmuseumofhistory.org/

Slave Life in Colonial America
www.benjaminschool.com/lower/hagy1/slave_life.htm

The Jamestown Colony
www.kidinfo.com/american.../colonization_jamestown.html

The Real Pocahontas
pocahontas.morenus.org/

INDEX

ABOUT THE AUTHOR AND THE CONSULTANT

Teresa LaClair is an author who lives in New York State, but she was born in Canada. She has also written other books for kids.

Dr. Jack N. Rakove is a professor of history and American studies at Stanford University, where he is director of American studies. The winner of the 1997 Pulitzer Prize in history, Dr. Rakove is the author of *The Unfinished Election of 2000, Constitutional Culture and Democratic Rule*, and *James Madison and the Creation of the American Republic*. He is also the president of the Society for the History of the Early American Republic.